This Journal Belongs To

_____

_____

_____

POTTER STYLE

© 2006 by Fiona Ellis.
Photographs of knitted cables on front
covers, page 1, meditation side bars, and
yoga bag © by Lindsey Maier.
Photographs of butterflies, sand ripples,
and trees © 2006 by Juniper Images and its
licensors. All rights reserved.
From the book *Inspired Cable Knits*
published by Potter Craft/Publishers,
Random House, Inc.
Yoga position illustrations by Katie Shaw.
www.clarksonpotter.com
ISBN-13: 978-0-307-34565-3
ISBN-10: 0-307-34565-3
Printed in China

Introduction

In our culture, we are bombarded by messages telling us to take time to relax and unwind. Isn't it strange that we need to be reminded? Taking time for ourselves is something pleasurable rather than a chore, so it should be an easy sell. Yet, we have become conditioned to feel guilty if we are not always achieving something.

Is knitting so popular because it is both relaxing and productive? In days gone by, knitting was only seen as work. Today, we understand both its meditative aspect and its ability to induce relaxation.

This journal has been created to address the contemplative nature of knitting. In addition to lined and graph paper pages for sketching designs and jotting down project notes, you will find meditations and mindfulness pointers scattered throughout. Although meditation is a highly personal experience, beginners may find it helpful to be directed by prompts from an instructor, to focus on each breath, for example. The mindfulness pointers in this journal are designed to mimic that process, bringing a higher level of focus and inspiration to both your knitting and your writing. As you write in this journal, you may discover that delving inward to observe, and describe, how your knitting develops can be a valuable tool in your path to self-discovery.

Finally, knitting is a physical activity; energy and materials are combined to create something tangible and new. Those who practice yoga are particularly aware of the powerful ways that energy is transferred through the mind and body. In the spirit of forging a mind-body connection through a physical, meditative activity, this journal contains a few special features in the back: a knitting pattern for a yoga mat bag and some suggested yoga stretches for knitters.

. . .

Putting Down Roots

There is a sense of both expectation and anticipation when we plant a seed. This is followed by a period where little appears to be happening, where we have to simply trust in the process. This is akin to casting on that initial row at the beginning of a knitting project. We know that the first few rows will go slowly while we learn the pattern and get into a rhythm, like a seed germinating. Just as an ugly bulb or dry, uninspiring seed eventually delights us when it blooms, these rows will come to fruition as the pattern reveals itself. Often, the cast-on edge can hardly be detected, but the roots of the pattern are certainly there.

Mindfulness pointer: Don't rush a seed

Pay attention to the first few rows of each piece; they contain the blueprint for the pattern. Without first putting down strong roots, nothing can grow. Remember, you would never rush a seed to come to fruition before it was time. Instead, you take delight in the anticipation of the beauty to come. So don't rush the foundation of your project. Enjoy watching it miraculously transform before your eyes into a beautiful pattern.

HAVE YOU EVER BEEN IMPATIENT TO GET BEYOND THE FIRST FEW ROWS OF A PROJECT? HOW DO YOU RELATE TO THIS POINTER?

Mindfulness pointer: The rhythm of the seasons

Consider how each part of the pattern feels. Does the last row of a repeat feel like you are coming full circle, only to begin the process all over again, just as a gardener might when planting bulbs or raking up leaves each year? Does the purl row feel like the dormancy of winter, a necessary fallowness in order to have the beauty of the spring that will follow?

HAVE YOU DISCOVERED ANY OTHER RHYTHMS OR REPETITIONS IN YOUR KNITTING THAT INSPIRE OR RELAX YOU?

Inspired by time

Our most precious commodity, next to love, may well be time. We all yearn to have more time, either to get more work done, to spend time with friends and family, to participate in favorite hobbies, or to just relax. Time may be a man-made invention, simply a tool for measurement, but it is a powerful force in our lives. The power of time is curious; when we are fully engrossed in doing something we love, time is the last thing on our minds.

Mindfulness pointer: Marking time

If you are like most knitters, you probably prefer to put your knitting down once you reach a particular point in the pattern, like reading to the end the chapter. But with knitting there are more options for stopping—it could be the end of a row or a pattern repeat. Try experimenting, stop at the same point in a pattern every time when working on one piece, then stop at a different point each time on another piece. Does one way feel easier? Which way adds to the relaxation and enjoyment your knitting brings you?

NOTES AFTER TRYING THIS EXERCISE:

Evolving Traditions

Most families create their own traditions to mark holidays and celebrations. But the traditions that we cling to are always evolving, just as our families themselves are always changing. Sometimes changes take place slowly and are hardly perceived. Others are more dramatic, and when they occur they cause us to create brand-new traditions, simply because it is no longer possible to continue with what has gone before.

As knitters we are acutely aware of the traditions present in the craft, which slowly become ingrained in our psyche through the act of repetition. We are linked—both to the past and to those yet to discover our craft—by the thread of current practice. We are part of a continuum.

Mindfulness pointer: Get in touch

How well developed is your sense of touch? Can you feel a change in the pattern as the piece slides through your hands, before you even see it? Try closing your eyes and find out if you can knit by feel alone. Just imagine all of the things you can do if you hone this skill: chat with friends or watch your favorite TV program while knitting. If you are not an experienced knitter, try this on the simple sections of a pattern.

THOUGHTS AFTER TRYING THIS EXERCISE:

Inspired by Touch

We use our senses to enjoy and understand the world. Knitters probably rely most heavily on sight and touch. We use sight in the initial choice of project and yarn, but the feel of the fiber also plays a huge part in its selection. Not only are we going to be touching every inch of our yarn as we make up the garment, but most times it will be touching our skin when the garment is worn.

Mindfulness Pointer: Let it flow

There are many times during a project when you may encounter an obstacle—the yarn store doesn't have the color you wanted, you want to complete a pattern repeat but are too tired, or you had hoped to finish the project to wear to your friend's wedding but you have run out of time. If obstacles do present themselves, try to accept the options that are open to you. Pay attention to the reactions you have. Would it make you feel better to let go of a sense of control and simply go with the flow?

CAN YOU APPLY THIS MINDFULNESS POINTER TO AN OBSTACLE IN YOUR KNITTING, OR MAYBE EVEN TO LIFE IN GENERAL?

Practice Makes Perfect

The more we practice a skill or technique, the better we become, no matter how accomplished we are to begin with. During our practice, usually at the very moment when we believe we are getting the hang of something, we goof. Don't think of this as a step backward; it's a retracing of the path. We have learned something since the last time so it is more like climbing a spiral staircase: After we complete one rotation, the view is almost the same—but not quite.

Mindfulness pointer: Knitting with intent

Try deciding what your intentions for a project are as you begin. Have an intention for how great you will look wearing it, how happy the recipient of the gift will be, how great you will feel having learned a new technique. As you work the first few rows, the intention will become set into the fabric as you learn the pattern. As you progress, how does it feel to keep returning to the pattern? Some days you may be less enthused. But avoiding the project is like eating a huge piece of chocolate cake when you were on the road to losing those ten extra pounds. Remember your intentions and get back to the pattern tomorrow. Before you know it, your intentions will be fulfilled.

THINK ABOUT YOUR CURRENT PROJECT. WHAT ARE YOUR INTENTIONS FOR IT?

Friendships develop from fragments of time two people spend together, some long and lingering, some short and snatched. But all are necessary to build a friendship.

When we unexpectedly bump into a friend, it brightens our day, makes us smile, and adds a little detail to the friendship. Similarly, each stitch builds on the one that came before, becoming first a row, and eventually a whole sweater.

Mindfulness pointer: Spiral learning

An experienced knitter is somebody who has made many mistakes, and—more important—continues to do so, constantly challenging herself or himself with a chosen project. If you make a mistake while working on a project, use it as an opportunity to watch your reactions. If you do work up the project without errors, then congratulate yourself on having practiced sufficiently and on having made enough mistakes previously to have achieved this level of skill.

ARE YOU EASILY ABLE TO REFRAME ERRORS AS AN OPPORTUNITY TO LEARN? IF NOT, THINK ABOUT PAST MISTAKES AND TRY TO RECALL ANY NEW SKILLS THAT WERE GAINED BY REWORKING THEM.

The Comfort of Friendship

We have all experienced a project that we began with great excitement only to later put it aside because something else came along. As you start on a project, resolve to spend time with your "friend," even if it is just for a few rows a day. Those stolen moments eventually add up, becoming more than the sum of their parts. Each day, remind yourself that comfort of friendship is right there waiting for you—just pick up the needles!

Mindfulness pointer: Energy stores

Have you ever noticed that yarn seems to come with its own supply of potential energy? In the spinning process, fibers are twisted together into yarn by means of electrical (or human) power. This power is converted to the tension stored within the strand of yarn. Your energy is then infused into a piece during the act of knitting. You will notice this if you have to rip out your knitting—the shapes of the stitches you formed still remain in the kinks of the yarn. You can see all this stored energy the moment you open your knitting basket and your knitting springs out, making a bid for freedom. So never underestimate the power of a hand-knitted sweater!

THINK ABOUT THE HANDMADE GIFTS THAT YOU'VE RECEIVED. DO YOU BELIEVE THAT A KNITTED GARMENT OR BLANKET CARRIES THE ENERGY OF THE PERSON WHO MADE IT?

Knitting Glossary

GARTER RIDGE: 2 or more knit rows following stockinette stitch or reverse stockinette stitch.

GARTER STITCH: Knit all rows.

REVERSE STOCKINETTE STITCH: Purl right side rows; knit wrong side rows (reverse of stockinette stitch).

SEED STITCH: When worked over an odd number of stitches, row 1: (k1, p1) to last stitch, end k1. Row 2: repeat row 1. When worked over an even number of stitches, row 1: (k1, p1) to end. Row 2: (p1, k1) to end.

STOCKINETTE STITCH: Knit on right-side rows; purl on wrong-side rows.

WORK EVEN: Continue working without increasing or decreasing stitches.

Needle Conversion Chart

METRIC	U.S. SIZES	CANADIAN/ U.K. SIZES
10	15	000
9	13	00
8	11	0
7.5	—	1
7	—	2
6.5	10.5	3
6	10	4
5.5	9	5
5	8	6
4.5	7	7
4	6	8
3.75	5	9
3.5	4	—
3.25	3	10
3	—	11
2.75	2	12
2.25	1	13
2	0	14
1.75	—	15

Abbreviations

ALT: alternate

APPROX: approximate(ly)

BEG: beginning

BO: bind off

C: cable

CB: center back

CF: center front

CM: centimeters

CN: cable needle

COLOR A, B, ETC.: indicates contrast colors

CONT: continue(ing)

DEC: decrease

DPN: double-pointed needle

FOLL: following

IN: inch(es)

INC: increase

INC 2: increase 2 stitches by working k1, p1, k1 all into next stitch

K: knit

K2TOG: knit 2 stitches together

K2TOGB: knit 2 stitches together through back of loops

LH: left-hand (as in "left-hand needle")

LHS: left-hand side

M1: make 1 stitch by picking up the strand between the next 2 stitches

M/C: main color

P: purl

PB: purl through back of loop

P2TOG: purl 2 stitches together

P2TOGB: purl 2 stitches together through back of loop

P3TOG: purl 3 stitches together

PATT(S): pattern(s)

PSSO: pass slipped stitch over

REM: remaining

REP: repeat

REV ST ST: reverse stockinette stitch, purl on right side rows, knit on wrong side rows

RH: right-hand (as in "right-hand needle")

RHS: right-hand side

RND(S): round(s)

RS: right side

SL: slip

SL2KNITWISE-K1-P2SSO: slip 2 stitches together as if to knit, knit next stitch from LH needle, pass both slipped stitches together over knitted stitch

SSK: slip next 2 stitches one at a time knitwise onto right needle; then knit them together in that position using left needle and working through front of loops

ST(S): stitch(es)

ST ST: stockinette stitch, knit on right side rows, purl on wrong side rows

T: twist

TBL: through back of loop

TOG: together

WS: wrong side

YB: yarn back

YFON: bring yarn forward and over needle

YFWD: yarn forward

YO: yarn over

YRN: yarn

*: designates the starting point for a repetition of a series of instructions

( ): alternative measurements or instructions

Tree-Pose Yoga Bag

*Y*oga practice has many facets. Once the body is properly aligned, energy flows more easily. This flow can be gained physically when practicing yoga, or mentally by cleansing the mind of distraction. When the mind is quieted, distractions and technical limitations no

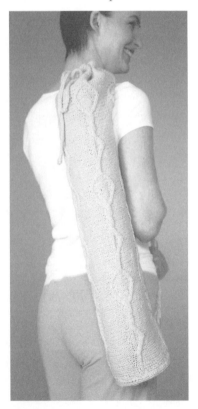

longer overpower the creative process. Ideas flow smoothly and abundantly.

FINISHED SIZE
Bag will measure 26.5 in [67 cm] long and 14 in [35.5 cm] in circumference.

MATERIALS
Hemp/Wool Yarn from Lana Knits, shade Natural, three 4 oz balls.

Pair of 3.5 mm needles, pair of 3.5 mm dpns, CN, cardboard to make inner base.

Yarn amount is based on average requirements and is approximate.

SOURCE

Lana Knits
Suite 3B, 320 Vernon Street
Nelson BC
Canada VII. 4E4
tel: 1.888.301.0011
www.hempforknitting.com

TENSION / GAUGE

24 sts and 28 rows = 4 in [10 cm] over stockinette stitch.

Take the time to check your gauge; change needle sizes if necessary to obtain correct gauge and garment size.

TECHNIQUES

I-CORDS: I-cords are made using a pair of double-pointed needles (dpns). Cast on the required number of stitches and knit them. *Do not turn the needle. Simply slide the stitches to the opposite end of needle, pull the yarn across the back of the stitches, and knit them once more.* Repeat from * to * until desired length.

A strand will be produced on the wrong side (WS), but as you work, you will see that each end of the rows will curl toward each other to form a tube and enclose this strand.

SHORT ROWS: Short rows are used for shaping. As you work across the row, the instructions will tell you to work a certain number of stitches. Wrap the next stitch, which prevents a hole from forming. Then turn the work, leaving the remaining stitches unworked, which are described as being "held."

To wrap a stitch: work to turn point; with yarn in back, slip the next stitch purlwise to the right-hand (RH) needle; bring yarn to front and then slip the same stitch back onto the LH needle. Turn work and bring yarn into position for next stitch, wrapping the stitch as you do. When you work across all the stitches once

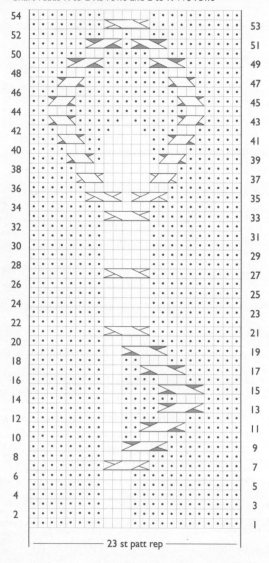

— 23 st patt rep —

SYMBOLS KEY:

	C3B	Slip next st onto CN & hold at back; k2 from LH needle; then k1 from CN
	C3F	Slip next 2 sts onto CN & hold at front, k1 from LH needle; then k2 from CN
	T3B	Slip next st onto CN & hold at back, k2 from LH needle; then p1 from CN
	T3F	Slip next 2 sts onto CN & hold at front, p1 from LH needle; then k2 from CN
	C4B	Slip next 2 sts onto CN & hold at back, k2 from LH needle; then k2 from CN
	C4F	Slip next 2 sts onto CN & hold at front, k2 from LH needle; then k2 from CN
	T4B	Slip next 2 sts onto CN & hold at back, k2 from LH needle; then p2 from CN
	T4F	Slip next 2 sts onto CN & hold at front, p2 from LH needle; then k2 from CN
	C5B	Slip next 2 sts onto CN & hold at back, k3 from LH needle; then k2 from CN
	C5F	Slip next 3 sts onto CN & hold at front, k2 from LH needle; then k3 from CN
	T5R	Slip next 2 sts onto CN & hold at back, k3 from LH needle; then p2 from CN
	T5L	Slip next 3 sts onto CN & hold at front, p2 from LH needle; then k3 from CN
•		p on RS; k on WS
☐		k on RS; p on WS

again, it is necessary to pick up the wraps to prevent them from showing on the right side (RS) of the fabric.

Picking up wraps: work to the stitch that is wrapped; insert tip of RH needle from the front under the wrap from bottom up and then into the wrapped stitch as usual. Knit them together, making sure the new stitch comes out under the wrap.

CABLE PATTERN

Row 1 (RS): p12, k3, p8.
Row 2: k8, p3, k12.
Rows 3–6: reps rows 1 and 2 twice.
Row 7: p10, C5B, p8.
Row 8: k8, p5, k10.
Row 9: p8, T5R, k2, p8.
Row 10: k8, p2, k2, p3, k8.
Row 11: p6, T5R, p2, k2, p8.
Row 12: k8, p2, k4, p3, k6.
Row 13: p4, T5R, p4, k2, p8.
Row 14: k8, p2, k6, p3, k4.
Row 15: p4, T5L, p4, k2, p8.
Row 16: rep row 12.
Row 17: p6, T5L, p2, k2, p8.
Row 18: rep row 10.
Row 19: p8, T5L, k2, p8.
Row 20: rep row 8.
Row 21: p10, C5F, p8.
Row 22: rep row 8.
Row 23: p10, k5, p8.
Rows 24 and 25: rep rows 22 and 23.
Rows 26–34: rep rows 20–25, then rows 20–22 once more.
Row 35: p8, C4B, k1, C4F, p6.
Row 36: k6, p9, k8.
Row 37: p7, C3B, k5, C3F, p5.
Row 38: k5, p11, k7.
Row 39: p6, T3B, p1, k5, p1, T3F, p4.
Row 40: k4, p2, k2, p5, k2, p2, k6.
Row 41: p5, T3B, p2, k5,

p2, T3F, p3.

Row 42: k3, p2, k4, p3, k4, p2, k5.

Row 43: p4, T3B, p5, k1, p5, T3F, p2.

Row 44: k2, p2, k13, p2, k4.

Row 45: p4, T3F, p11, T3B, p2.

Row 46: k3, p2, k11, p2, k5.

Row 47: p5, T3F, p9, T3B, p3.

Row 48: k4, p2, k9, p2, k6.

Row 49: p6, T4F, p5, T4B, p4.

Row 50: k6, p2, k5, p2, k8.

Row 51: p8, T4F, p1, T4B, p6.

Row 52: k8, p2, k1, p2, k10.

Row 53: rep row 21.

Row 54: rep row 8.

Rep rows 1–54 for patt.

BAG

Using 3.5 mm needles, cast on 92 sts (this is bottom of bag).

Work 1 row in seed st.

RS row: (work 23 st patt rep row 1 of chart) 4 times.

WS row: (work 23 st patt rep row 2 of chart) 4 times.

Rep these 2 rows twice more. Cable panels are now set.

Cont working rows 3–54, followed by rows 1–54 twice more as set.

Then cont working rows 1 and 2 of chart until piece measures 25 in [63.5 cm] from beg.

Knit 8 rows to form garter band.

Eyelet row: k7, *yfon, k2tog, k5, rep from * to last st, k1.

Purl 1 row, knit 8 rows. BO all sts.

BASE

Using 3.5 mm needles, cast on 14 sts, purl 1 row.

work first triangle as follows:
RS row: k13, wrap next st, turn, leave rem st unworked in hold.

WS: p13.

Next RS row: k12, wrap next st, turn, 2 sts now in hold. WS: p12.

Next RS row: k11, wrap next st, turn, 3 sts now in hold. WS: p11.

Cont in this way leaving an additional st in hold each RS row until the following 2 rows have been completed: RS row: k1, wrap next st, turn 13 sts now in hold and WS row: p1.

Knit across all sts picking up wraps.

work second triangle as follows:
WS row: p13, wrap next st, turn, leave rem st unworked in hold.

RS: k13.

Next WS row: p12, wrap next st, turn, 2 sts now in hold. RS: k12.

Next WS row: p11, wrap next st, turn, 3 sts now in hold. RS: k11.

Cont in this way leaving an additional st in hold each WS row until the following 2 rows have been completed: WS row: p1, wrap next st, turn, 13 sts now in hold and RS row: k1.

Purl across all sts picking up wraps. Knit 1 row.

Work third triangle as given for second triangle.

Work fourth triangle as given for second triangle.

Work fifth triangle as given for second triangle.

BO all sts. Sew bind-off edge to side of first triangle to form a circle.

STRAPS

Using pair of 3.5 mm dpns, make 3 4-stitch I-cords 26 in [66 cm] long and 1 4-stitch I-cord 40 in [101.5 cm] long.

FELTING

Place base and I-cords in a small laundry bag and place in washing machine with a few larger items (I suggest 2–3 pairs of jeans). Wash on hot with a cold rinse cycle using mild laundry soap. Block out pieces to dry. Base should now measure 5.5 in [14 cm] in diameter, if it is still larger than this, rep wash cycle until desired size is achieved.

FINISHING

Block bag piece to given dimensions. Join seam to make a tube. Sew base to bottom of bag.

Braid the 3 shorter I-cords together to make strap, secure ends together by sewing. Stitch strap in position, on seam where seam meets the base, and at the top just below the first garter band.

Thread longer I-cord through eyelets, beg and end at point opposite from seam. Knot ends to prevent slipping through holes during use.

make the inner base:
Cut a 5.5 in [14 cm] diameter circle from cardboard and place in the bottom of bag to reinforce.

Place yoga mat in bag, draw up cord to close opening, and tie. Take along to your next yoga class, trying not to allow your ego to be too proud.

Yoga Poses for Knitters

*The Eagle Pose (left) and Triangle Pose (right)
help open up the shoulders.*

*The Child's Pose
eases tired shoulders and neck.*

*The Downward Dog
lengthens the spine.*

The Shoulder Stand
brings blood flow back to the brain.

A backbend pose, such as the Bridge,
counters the hours spent with a rounded back.

The Tree Pose
was the inspiration for the yoga mat bag pattern.

ALSO BY FIONA ELLIS

Inspired Cable Knits:
20 Creative Designs for Making Sweaters and Accessories

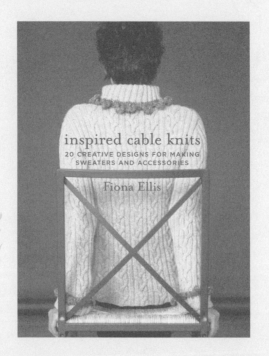

inspired cable knits
20 CREATIVE DESIGNS FOR MAKING
SWEATERS AND ACCESSORIES

Fiona Ellis

ISBN: 1-4000-8271-4
$35.00 hardcover (Canada: $50.00)